BizAwareness.com

Common Sense to Starting and Running Your Business

Forrest Ketner

Welcome to BizAwareness.com

I am not going to tell you if you follow this report you can make 6 to 7 figure income like some other people do, but this is common sense and helpful advice on starting and running your business. In this report you will find helpful advice even some advice that will save you thousands of dollars. Your income will only be limited by the amount you put into building and increasing your business, when you hit six figures please send me a thank you note.

This report is written to help you not make some costly mistakes and to encourage you to get started and do what you love. When you work for yourself you can set your own hours, honestly this usually means you will find more time to work so you can increase your earnings. If you need a day off you can schedule yourself the one you want.

It may not be easy to start but that is why this report gives you helpful advice. After 30 years of running my own businesses and years in management, and retail sales I am glad to help you not make some costly mistakes.

Subscribe to our monthly newsletter and get your questions answered.

Subscribe to our monthly newsletter and we will answer your questions every month. The way this will work is you will have to contact us through www.BizAwareness.com by the 14th of the month to be in the next month's newsletter. This will give me 2 weeks to get the newsletter together and then you will be notified by the 5th of month so you can download your own copy. In the newsletter we will not have your name but will use your question and your initials, and then provide you with a common sense answer.

Subscribe to the newsletter on BizAwareness.com and you can cancel at anytime.

If you have any questions about the report or

the newsletter use the contact form on our

website and we will be glad to give you an

answer.

Who Should Start a Business

Who should start a business? I would suggest anybody that wants to. It could be a small business, online, service, tutoring, brick and mortar, business to business, the sky is the limit you could even sale kites at the beach. The feeling of having your own business is well worth the planning and starting.

Some people even fall into a business by working to the top and then inheriting or buying the business, if this is the case you still need to make a plan to run the business to its potential.

Think it through and make a plan and then work the plan to its maximum.

You don't want to get ten years down the road and wonder how it would have been to have your own business. You can start a business relatively inexpensive and run it and let it expand. I started my ebay business by selling 3 hub caps off of my van, one fell off while driving and was never found. So I took off the other 3 and sold them on ebay for $80, taking that amount and buying some new mens ties for $50. Some of those ties sold for 20 to 35 dollars each, and I continued to build my inventory until I was listing 500 pieces in my ebay store.

You may be able to start a service business by doing a couple jobs with rented equipment and then buy the equipment or tools that you need. The common sense principal here would be to not get a loan and then try to turn a profit while paying for the loan.

You actually don't need to know exactly what you're doing to get started. Think of some of the greats like Columbus, Einstein, Steve Jobs and more, they didn't have an exact plan for the course but they had an idea and chased after it. So get started and see where your path leads you,

always treat your customer as you would like to be treated

and stay professional.

What is needed to start a business

What is needed to start a business first thing would be customers, somebody needs to buy or need what you have to offer. You will need a product or service that has a need.

The best way to let someone know you are in business are business cards, these are a cheap way to get the word out and then after your first batch of customers word of mouth will kick in and help grow your business. I would highly suggest making your business cards part of your marketing and put an offer, or your referral program on the back of them. This way your business cards can create more business rather than just carrying your phone number and address.

Where to start your business

You will need a location it could be a spare room or closet if your business is online, it may be you vehicle, car, van or truck I still use a mobile office meaning using my vehicle while working. Maybe your business requires an office, or retail location known as brick and mortar. Start out small and build the business, don't let the rent and utilities get ahead of your business.

How much room is needed? Maybe you just needed a computer for an online business, you might just need a tool bag, or a chef may need his knife pouch. A chef could work for a family or business and provide their daily meals.

You could clean carpets or provide cleaning services for families these would not require a truck or a whole lot of equipment. A handy man may require more diverse tools or could limit himself to just a couple specialties. The space neede in your home could just be a desk, or a laptop, and maybe a shelf or two.

The problem here is not knowing what you need but after a job or two you will start collecting your supplies if you don't have them already. If you went from a hobby to a business you probably already have what you need. Take the first jov and get started and the others that follow will flow along better and will get completed quicker.

Maybe you have been looking for a job, you could make your own and do what you love. Consider all the time spent filling out job applications, you could have spent all that time making money.

When to start your business?

When to start your business? The answer would be now is the time, no better time than the present. Just start I believe in failing fast, it is much better to start and fail and go on to the next business instead of taking years to analyze and start.

What about the economy? The economy will never be perfect and if you wait for that time it will never arrive. There will always be people willing to pay someone else to improve their lives or their families.

Bonus 33 Business ideas you can use

If you brain has stalled and you don't know what business

you would like to start here are lots of ideas for you and

there are many more possibilities.

1. Online store
2. Painter
3. Faux Painter
4. Website builder
5. Junk hauler
6. Mow lawns
7. Tech help
8. Pig bar b que
9. Handyman
10. Car detailer
11. Carpet cleaning
12. Private chef
13. Locksmith

14. Install blinds

15. Drywall Patcher

16. Dog walker

17. Clean out attics, basements

18. Uber driver

19. Guitar/ Piano lessons

20. Foreign language tutor

21. Flower arranging

22. Baby sitting

23. Cleaning/ maid

24. Custom window treatments

25. Rent chickens

26. Build sheds/ dog houses

27. Landscaping

28. Concrete ornaments

29. Wallpaper

30. Facebook classified

31. eBay

32. Etsy

33. Craigslist

Seven things you may need to start your business.

1. Business cards

2. Website

3. Email account

4. Phone

5. Advertising

6. Permits/Insurance/Sales Tax

7. Checking account

Save thousands of dollars

Method one for saving thousands of dollars.

Don't make the mistake of turning your website over to a web designer. You can save thousands on your website by doing it yourself or hiring a high school kid part time, or maybe you have a younger family member that would be more than capable of setting up your website.

You can save thousands of dollars doing it this way.

Your website doesn't have to be perfect it just needs your business name and contact information. Add a photo or two. I would recommend Godaddy.com. I have had websites that I have made since 1997 when we had to wait for dial up.

The problems you will have if you turn your website over to a designer will be if you need to change something, you are at their mercy and timeline. Also the rice they charge

could be $3000 and higher. Right now you are starting and

should be reinvesting your money to grow your business.

Websites do not start attracting people to you

immediately they take some time and more money to be

added to the search engines. You can attract people to

your website by putting the address on your business card.

Method two for saving thousands of dollars.

You could spends thousands of dollars on advertising, I

once had a small Yellow Page ad that cost me $1800 for

the year and it did not draw more than a few customers.

You can advertise cheap and local on Facebook or Craiglist. I have had more success with Facebook than with Craiglist, start a business Facebook page and then you can advertise locally in radius miles of your location for as cheap as one dollar a day.

I have had some success with a newspaper classified ad but they are more costly around $50 for a day or two, check with your local paper if you are interested. But I would suggest trying Facebook first.

These two pages could save you upwards of ten thousand dollars.

What kind of Business Entity should I use? Licensing and Permits?

I would suggest just starting as a sole proprietor until your business gets bigger than maybe and incorporation or LLC. There is a lot more paper work needed and accounting if your form an INC or LLC.

Seek legal advice on this I am not a lawyer or an accountant.

Licensing each state has different business license requirements, check with your local state and even with your local governments they may also require business licenses. Licenses are required for certain vocations or occupations that may be conducted within a business.

Employer Identification Number (EIN) – Taxpayer

Identification Number Generally, an EIN is required by the

IRS if: 1) The business will have employees; and/or 2) the

business operates as a corporation or partnership.

Business Insurance Contact an insurance agent to

determine the types of insurance the business should

purchase. Shop around. Insurance rates and types of

coverage vary greatly among insurance carriers. I currently

carry an Artisan policy that gives me coverage of one

million dollars, this policy costs about $450 a year.

Zoning and Local Requirements: It is important for starting
and expanding businesses to make sure that the planned
location or occupied facility is in compliance with all the
local laws and regulations.

Branding my theory on this is save your money, if you are
not Coke, or Kleenex it will costs you hundreds of
thousands of dollars to have your name become this
popular and known.

Business Plans

A simple outline is about all you need unless you are
forming a corporation or partnership with employees.
Include your mission, vision and marketing ideas with
some goals for your income.

Many entrepreneurs get bogged down in their need for a
full business plan to start their businesses, some even
spend money to have somebody else write one for them.
Make an outline and use the KISS method, Keep It Simple
Stupid.

New Company Setup Checklist

COMPANY INFORMATION	
Company name:	
Address:	
Telephone number:	
Fax number:	
Date business started:	
Number of owners:	

CHECKLIST		
☐	Choose type of business entity. Business entity type: [Sole Proprietorship/LLC/Corporation]	
☐	Select end of fiscal year. Fiscal year-end: December 31,	
☐	Apply for IRS Employer Identification Number (EIN), if applicable.	To obtain Form SS-4 to apply for an EIN, go to irs.gov

BizAwareness.com

- [ ] Register with state as a business.
- [ ] Obtain county and city business licenses.
- [ ] If corporation, file letters of incorporation. If partnership, create and sign partnership agreement.
- [ ] Purchase insurance plan(s).
- [ ] Create company Web site. Web site address:
- [ ] Choose an accounting method:
- [ ] Open a business banking account.
- [ ] Obtain a business credit card.
- [ ] Consider contracting with payroll processing firm and/or record-keeping firm.
- [ ] Establish a salary agreement for each owner.

Business Cards what to include.

You can only make a first impression one time let your

cards make a great impression. Here is what you should

put on your business cards.

1. **Name**

2. **Address**

3. **Phone**

4. **Website**

5. **Email**

6. **Slogan if you have one**

7. **Facebook twitter address if you use them**

8. **Use the back for a coupon or a referral program**

Here are some mistakes to avoid on your cards.

1. **Font too small not everybody has perfect vision**

2. **Font too light in color matching the background**

3. **No email or website address**

4. **Printed on cheap paper**

5. **Back side blank I use the back for my referral program**

Any trademarks, service marks, product names, or named features are assumed to be the property of their respective owners, and are used only for reference. There is no implied endorsement if we use one of these terms.

Finally, use your head. Nothing in this Guide is intended to replace common sense, legal, medical or other professional advice, and is meant to inform and entertain the reader.